SMALL PRIVATE GARDENS

teNeues

Editor and texts:	Alejandro Bahamón
Copy editing:	Cristina Doncel
Layout:	Cris Tarradas, Oriol Serra Juncosa
Translations:	Ana Cañizares (English), Susanne Engler (German), Marion Westerhoff (French), Alessandro Orsi (Italian)

Produced by Loft Publications
www.loftpublications.com

Published by teNeues Publishing Group

teNeues Publishing Company
16 West 22nd Street, New York, NY 10010, USA
Tel.: 001-212-627-9090, Fax: 001-212-627-9511

teNeues Book Division
Kaistraße 18
40221 Düsseldorf, Germany
Tel.: 0049-(0)211-994597-0, Fax: 0049-(0)211-994597-40

teNeues Publishing UK Ltd.
P.O. Box 402
West Byfleet
KT14 7ZF, Great Britain
Tel.: 0044-1932-403509, Fax: 0044-1932-403514

teNeues France S.A.R.L.
4, rue de Valence
75005 Paris, France
Tel.: 0033-1-55 76 62 05, Fax: 0033-1-55 76 64 19

teNeues Iberica S.L.
Pso. Juan de la Encina 2-48, Urb. Club de Campo
28700 S.S.R.R., Madrid, Spain
Tel./Fax: 0034-916 595 876

www.teneues.com

ISBN-10:	3-8327-9075-6
ISBN-13:	978-3-8327-9075-2

© 2006 teNeues Verlag GmbH + Co. KG, Kempen

Printed in Spain

Bibliographic information published by
Die Deutsche Bibliothek. Die Deutsche Bibliothek lists
this publication in the Deutsche Nationalbibliografie;
detailed bibliographic data is available in the Internet
at http://dnb.ddb.de.

VEGETATION

10–39

ARCHITECTURE

40–81

FURNITURE

82–107

WATER

108–135

INTRODUCTION

EINLEITUNG

INTRODUCTION

INTRODUCCIÓN

INTRODUZIONE

The private garden has existed since the outset of architecture, and has always been perceived as a space that provides those who enjoy it with the thrill of exerting a certain control over nature. During the formation of large and densely populated urban centers over the last decades, the concept of the traditional garden has undergone a radical transformation and come to be an ideal space exclusive to the wealthiest sectors. The need for man to control nature and own a piece, however small, of the precious Garden of Eden is reflected in a new typology that is scattered around the most remote corners of our cities: the small private garden. The owners of these spaces manage to turn flaw into virtue by creating gardens where there was scarcely any space for them. This selection gathers some of the most recent and significant small private gardens around the world, testifying to the evolution of the perception of this intimate space and displaying the solutions used by designers to achieve their conception.

Mit den Anfängen der Architektur entwickelte sich auch der private Garten, der stets als ein Bereich verstanden wurde, der denjenigen, die ihn nutzen, das Gefühl gibt, die Natur zu beherrschen. In den letzten Jahrzehnten entstanden große, dicht besiedelte Städte, die es mit sich brachten, dass sich das traditionelle Konzept des Gartens radikal gewandelt hat. Für viele Menschen ist der Garten ein fast unerfüllbarer Wunsch geworden, der den reicheren Gesellschaftsschichten vorbehalten bleibt. Das latente Verlangen des Menschen, die Natur zu beherrschen und einen Teil dieses kostbaren Garten Eden zu besitzen, wie klein dieser auch sein mag, spiegelt sich in einem neuen Typus, der in den verborgensten Winkeln unserer Städte entsteht: des kleinen Privatgartens. Oft sind dies Orte, an denen die Bewohner aus der Not eine Tugend gemacht haben, indem es ihnen gelang an Stellen Gärten anzulegen, wo eigentlich gar kein Platz dafür war. Dieses Buch stellt einige der neuesten und interessantesten kleinen Privatgärten weltweit vor, Zeugnisse der Entwicklung und des Wandels der Ideenkonzepte für diese intimen Bereiche, und es zeigt Gestaltungsmethoden, die Designer heute anwenden, um ihre Entwürfe umzusetzen.

Le jardin privé, de tout temps inséparable de l'architecture, a toujours été compris comme un espace donnant, à ceux qui en bénéficient, l'illusion d'exercer un pouvoir sur la nature. Au cours des dernières décennies, suite à la création des premiers grands centres urbains à forte densité de population, on a assisté à une transformation radicale du concept traditionnel de jardin en un lieu idéal et exclusif des classes plus aisées. Le besoin latent de l'homme de dominer la nature et de posséder une partie, aussi petite soit-elle, de ce précieux jardin d'Eden, se reflète dans une nouvelle typologie essaimée dans les plus petits recoins de nos villes : le jardin privé de petites dimensions. Ce sont souvent des endroits où les habitants ont essayé de transformer une surface inutilisé en petit coin de paradis, là même où l'espace semblait très limité. Cette collection offre une palette récente de petits jardins privés du monde entier, témoins de l'évolution au niveau de la compréhension de ce paysage si intime, et nous montre l'art et la manière des paysagistes pour les moduler.

El jardín privado ha acompañado a la arquitectura desde sus orígenes y siempre se ha entendido como un espacio que proporciona a quienes lo disfrutan la ilusión de ejercer un dominio sobre la naturaleza. En las últimas décadas, desde que se empezaron a formar grandes asentamientos urbanos densamente poblados, se ha asistido a una transformación radical del concepto tradicional de jardín, que se ha convertido en el lugar ideal y exclusivo de las clases más adineradas. La necesidad latente del hombre de dominar la naturaleza y de poseer una parte, por pequeña que sea, de ese preciado jardín del Edén se refleja en una nueva tipología que salpica los más recónditos rincones de nuestras ciudades: el jardin privado de dimensiones reducidas. Son lugares en los que sus habitantes han intentado hacer de un defecto una virtud y han logrado construir jardines donde apenas había espacio para ellos. Esta compilación, que recoge algunos de los más recientes y significativos ejemplos de pequeños jardines privados de todo el mundo, muestra la evolución de una manera de entender este paisaje tan íntimo así como las herramientas que emplean los diseñadores para su construcción.

Il giardino privato ha accompagnato l'architettura fin dalle sue origini e da sempre si è considerato uno spazio che offre, a coloro che ne godono i benefici, l'illusione di esercitare un dominio sulla natura. Negli ultimi decenni, da quando si sono iniziati a formare grandi insediamenti urbani densamente popolati, si è assistito ad una trasformazione radicale del concetto tradizionale di giardino, che si è trasformato nel luogo ideale ed esclusivo delle classi più abbienti. Il bisogno latente nell'uomo di dominare la natura e di entrare in possesso di una parte, per piccola che sia, di quel prezioso giardino dell'Eden, si rispecchia in una nuova tipologia che invade gli angoli più reconditi delle nostre città: il giardino privato di dimensioni ridotte. Sono luoghi in cui gli abitanti hanno cercato di fare di un difetto una virtù riuscendo a piantare dei giardini dove appena c'era spazio. Questa raccolta, che riunisce alcuni dei più recenti e significativi esempi di piccoli giardini privati di tutto il mondo, mostra l'evoluzione della maniera di intendere questo paesaggio così intimo e mostra i ferri del mestiere che impiegano i designer nel plasmarlo.

Vegetation
Vegetation
Vegetation
Vegetación
Vegetazione

Vegetation is the raw material needed to create any garden. In the case of small gardens within an urban context limited in terms of natural conditions, however, the vegetation should be carefully selected to respond not only to these conditions but also to the expectation of creating the illusion of a natural and protected environment. A variety of strategies exist to fill a confined area with vegetation, from planting creepers that grow over walls to planting grass as the primary element in order to unify the exterior space and emphasize its boundaries. In any case, and however modest, the vegetal element is essential in lending a natural character to these exterior urban areas. A less restrained approach that requires an especially careful selection of plants and an additional dose of dedication consists in creating a large mass of vegetation that invades a large part of the garden's surface area. This generates an effect of apparent depth and exuberance through the adequate placement of each of the plants.

Pflanzen sind das Grundelement zur Schaffung eines jeden Gartens. Wenn es sich jedoch um kleine Gärten in städtischer und eingeschränkter natürlicher Umgebung handelt, müssen die Pflanzen sorgfältig ausgewählt werden, damit sie sich an diese Voraussetzungen anpassen und doch die Illusion einer natürlichen und geschützten Umgebung entstehen lassen. Es können sehr verschiedene Methoden bei der Bepflanzung einer kleinen Fläche angewendet werden. Beispielsweise kann man eine Mauer mit Kletterpflanzen begrünen und dadurch einen vertikalen Garten schaffen, oder Rasen als Hauptelement wählen und so den Außenraum vereinheitlichen und seine Begrenzungen hervorheben. Die pflanzlichen Elemente, auch wenn sie noch so klein sind, sind auf jeden Fall unabdinglich, um einer Außenfläche in der Stadt den Charakter eines Gartens zu verleihen. Eine sehr wirksame Methode, die jedoch eine genaue Kenntnis des günstigsten Zeitpunktes für die Pflanzung der verschiedenen Gewächse und viel Hingabe bei der Arbeit erfordert, ist die Schaffung einer großen Anpflanzung, die den Großteil der als Garten genutzten Fläche bedeckt. Durch eine geschickte Kombination der Pflanzen erzielt man auf diese Weise den Eindruck von Tiefe und Üppigkeit.

La végétation est la matière première nécessaire à la création de tout jardin. Toutefois, au chapitre des jardins de taille réduite en environnement urbain, la végétation doit être soigneusement choisie pour répondre à ces limitations spatiales et au besoin de créer l'illusion d'un environnement naturel protégé. Les stratégies d'implantation végétale d'une petite enceinte sont très variées : installation de plantes grimpantes pour recouvrir un mur, créant ainsi un jardin vertical ou emploi du gazon comme élément protagoniste, unifiant ainsi l'espace extérieur pour en exalter les limites. Dans tous les cas, et aussi modeste soit-il, l'élément végétal est indispensable pour transformer en jardin ces zones urbaines extérieures. Une stratégie répandue, nécessitant une grande connaissance à l'heure de choisir les espèces et beaucoup de temps, consiste à créer une grande masse végétale sur la plus grande surface utile du jardin. C'est une façon d'obtenir un effet de profondeur et d'exubérance apparent grâce à une disposition adéquate de chaque espèce.

La vegetación es la materia prima en la creación de cualquier jardín; sin embargo, al tratarse de jardines reducidos, en entornos urbanos y condiciones naturales limitadas, la vegetación debe ser cuidadosamente escogida para que responda tanto a estas limitaciones como a los deseos de crear la ilusión de un entorno natural y protegido. Las estrategias para poblar un pequeño recinto con vegetación pueden ser muy variadas; desde plantar enredaderas para recubrir un muro y crear así un jardín en vertical hasta emplear el césped como elemento protagonista y, de este modo, unificar el espacio exterior y exaltar sus propios límites. En cualquier caso, y por modesto que sea, el elemento vegetal es imprescindible para otorgar un carácter ajardinado a estas zonas exteriores urbanas. Una estrategia contundente, pero que requiere un gran dominio a la hora de elegir las especies y una dosis adicional de dedicación, consiste en crear una gran masa de vegetación que invada la mayor parte de la superficie útil del jardín. De este modo, se consigue un efecto de profundidad y exuberancia aparentes, ya que se trata simplemente de una disposición adecuada de cada una de las especies.

La vegetazione è la materia prima con cui si crea qualsiasi giardino, tuttavia, visto che si tratta di giardini di dimensioni ridotte, situati in contesti urbani dove gli spazi naturali sono limitati, la vegetazione deve essere selezionata con attenzione perché possa rispondere sia a questi condizionamenti, sia al desiderio di creare l'illusione di un ambiente naturale e protetto. Le strategie con cui si può distribuire la vegetazione in un piccolo recinto possono essere molto diverse: dalle piante rampicanti, che ricoprano un muro per creare un giardino verticale, fino al prato come elemento protagonista, che renda lo spazio esterno uniforme e metta in risalto i propri limiti. Ad ogni modo, per modesto che sia, l'elemento vegetale è imprescindibile perché sia possibile conferire l'aspetto di un giardino a questi spazi urbani all'aria aperta. Una strategia efficace, che tuttavia richiede un gran dominio nella selezione delle specie e una dose addizionale di dedicazione, consiste nel creare una gran massa di vegetazione cha occupi la maggior parte della superficie utile del giardino; in questo modo, si ottiene un effetto di profondità ed esuberanza, sebbene apparenti, poiché è un'illusione prodotta dalla conveniente collocazione di ciascuna specie.

Dangar House

Landscape design: William Dangar & Associates
Location: Sydney, Australia
Photography: William Dangar, Murray Fredericks

The design of this garden emphasizes the spaciousness of the residence by using the same wooden floor used inside the home. A wide variety of plants make for a rich and exuberant space.

Die Gestaltung des Gartens lässt dieses Haus größer wirken, da für den Außenraum der gleiche Holzfußboden wie für Innen benutzt wurde. Die große Vielfalt des Pflanzenbewuchses schafft eine prächtige und zugleich üppige Atmosphäre.

Le design du jardin rehausse l'étendue de la maison grâce à l'emploi du même revêtement de bois à l'extérieur qu'à l'intérieur. La grande diversité d'espèces végétales permet de créer un espace riche et exubérant.

El diseño del jardín refuerza la amplitud de la casa al emplear el mismo pavimento de madera que en el interior. Una amplia variedad de vegetación permitió lograr un espacio rico y exuberante.

Il disegno del giardino mette in risalto la spaziosità della casa usando lo stesso pavimento di legno che è stato usato per gli interni. La scelta di una vegetazione variata ha permesso di ottenere uno spazio ricco ed esuberante.

Desert Space

Landscape design: Taylor Cullity Lethlean
Location: Adelaide, Australia
Photography: Taylor Cullity Lethlean

The "Desert Space" forms part of the garden belonging to the designers' residence. The scarce and scattered vegetation represents their interpretation of a journey through the desert.

Der „Desert Space" ist ein Teil des Gartens des Hauses der Designer selbst. Die spärliche und verstreute Vegetation ist die Interpretation einer Reise durch die Wüste.

Le « Desert Space » fait partie du jardin de la résidence des designers eux-mêmes. La végétation rare et éparse représente un voyage à travers le désert.

El "Desert Space" forma parte del jardín de la residencia de los propios diseñadores. La vegetación escasa y dispersa es una interpretación de un recorrido por el desierto.

Il "Desert Space" fa parte del giardino della dimora dei designer. La vegetazione rada e sparsa è la rappresentazione di un percorso nel deserto.

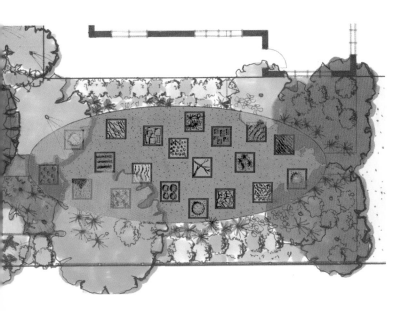

Ward Residence Garden

Lanscape design: Andrea Cochran
Location: Palo Alto, CA, United States
Photography: Andrea Cochran

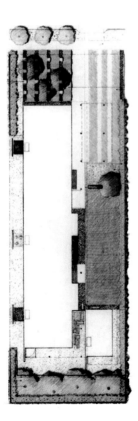

The design of this garden complements the modern and functionalist character of the residence. In order to obtain greater privacy, a relaxing and sculptural interior landscape was created through the implementatin of various plants.

Die Gestaltung dieses Gartens ergänzt den modernen und funktionellen Charakter des Hauses. Um eine größtmögliche Privatsphäre zu schaffen, wurde eine entspannende und skulptural wirkende Innenlandschaft angelegt, die durch eine vielfältige Vegetation geprägt ist.

La conception de ce jardin complète le caractère moderne et fonctionnel de la résidence. Pour obtenir une meilleure intimité, un paysage intérieur à la fois apaisant et sculptural a été créé à partir d'une végétation variée.

El diseño de este jardín complementa el carácter moderno y funcionalista de la residencia. Para conseguir una mayor privacidad se creó un paisaje interior relajado y escultural a partir de una variada vegetación.

Il disegno di questo giardino fa da complemento al carattere moderno e funzionalista della casa. Per ottenere una privacy maggiore si è creato, utilizzando una vegetazione variata, un paesaggio interiore rilassante e scultoreo.

Delray Beach Private Garden

Landscape design: Michael Singer
Location: Delray Beach, FL, United States
Photography: David Stansbury

Despite the reduced dimensions of this residential garden in Florida, the lavish tropical vegetation creates a sense of amplitude and depth.

Obwohl der Garten dieses Hauses in Florida sehr klein ist, entstand durch die üppige tropische Vegetation der Eindruck von Weite.

Malgré ses proportions réduites, le jardin de cette maison de Floride, doté d'une végétation tropicale exubérante, crée une sensation d'étendue.

A pesar de las reducidas proporciones del jardín de esta vivienda de Florida, la exuberante vegetación tropical crea una sensación de amplitud.

Malgrado le ridotte proporzioni di giardino di questa casa in Florida, l'esuberante vegetazione tropicale trasmette una sensazione di spaziosità.

Private Garden in Habikino

Landscape design: Akira Sakamoto/Casa, Toshiya Ogino
Location: Habikino-City, Japan
Photography: Masaru Kitamura

These three private gardens in the city of Habikino present a subtle and spontaneous design inspired by the existing vegetation and emphasized by the integration of delicate elements such as the grass.

Diese drei privaten Gärten in der Stadt Habikino sind sehr subtil gestaltet und wirken dadurch natürlich. Ausgehend von der bereits vorhandenen Vegetation, wurde ein Rasen als anmutiges Hauptgestaltungselement integriert.

Ces trois jardins privés situés dans la ville de Habikino présentent une conception subtile et spontanée, où la végétation est utilisée comme point de départ et où revient à un élément délicat comme la pelouse le rôle principal.

Estos tres jardines privados situados en la ciudad de Habikino presentan un diseño sutil y espontáneo, donde la vegetación existente se toma como punto de partida y un delicado elemento como el césped cobra gran protagonismo.

Questi tre giardini privati nella città di Habikino presentano un disegno delicato e spontaneo, dove la vegetazione esistente si prende come punto di partenza e dove un elemento fragile come il prato assume un gran rilievo.

Ivy Street Roof Garden

Landscape design: Andrea Cochran
Location: San Francisco, CA, United States
Photography: Andrea Cochran

This garden transforms the top floor of a building in San Francisco into an evocative landscape composed of small plantations contained within large, undulating boxes made of rusted iron sheets.

Dieser Garten verwandelt das letzte Stockwerk eines zentral gelegenen Gebäudes in San Francisco in eine eindrucksvolle Landschaft aus kleinen Pflanzengruppen, die in großen geschwungenen Kisten aus oxidierten Eisenblechen angeordnet sind.

Ce jardin métamorphose le dernier étage d'un immeuble au centre de San Francisco en un paysage suggestif composé de petites plantations installées dans de grands bacs en lames de fer oxydé et aux formes ondoyantes.

Este jardín convierte la última planta de un céntrico edificio de San Francisco en un sugerente paisaje de pequeñas plantaciones contenidas en grandes cajas ondulantes de láminas de hierro oxidado.

Questo giardino trasforma l'ultimo piano di un edificio del centro di San Francisco in un suggestivo paesaggio di piccole piantagioni, inserite in grandi casse ondulate composte da lamine di ferro ossidato.

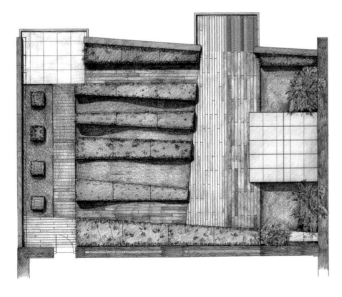

Private gardens, especially those with reduced surface areas and located mainly in urban contexts, experience a close relationship with architecture as a result of the latter's task in establishing the limits, structure and character of an exterior space. In relation to the garden's proportions and situation within the building, a variety of typologies that determine their subsequent function can be generated: garden, terrace, balcony, vertical gardens, patio, front garden, etc. However, given the inadequate conditions generated by our lack of time to look after the vegetation, a new typology exists today that can be applied to all the previous ones: a garden in which the architectural elements predominate over the vegetation. Through the integration of natural elements that generally require low maintenance, an architectural garden can be created on a formally and conceptually sound basis. If as anticipated, in little over a decade, at least half of the planet's population will inhabit urban centers, it is indeed quite probable that this type of garden will predominate in the future.

Private Gärten, und insbesondere sehr kleine Gärten, die meist in der Stadt liegen, sind eng mit der Architektur verbunden, die sie begrenzt, strukturiert und ihren Charakter prägt. Je nach der Größe und Lage innerhalb des Gebäudes unterscheidet man dabei verschiedene Arten, die von ihrer späteren Funktion abhängen: Gärten, Terrassen, Balkone, hängende Gärten, Höfe, Vorgärten usw. Da jedoch die Bedingungen zur Anlage eines Gartens nicht immer optimal sind und die stete Beschleunigung des Lebensrhythmus in der Stadt dem Menschen nur noch wenig Zeit lässt, einen Garten zu pflegen, setzt sich ein bestimmter Typ Garten immer mehr durch, der auf alle genannten Formen bezogen werden kann: Ein Garten, in dem leblose, architektonische Elemente die Natur überwiegen. Durch bestimmte pflanzliche Elemente, die im Allgemeinen wenig Pflege benötigen, wird ein architektonischer Garten geschaffen, in dem das formale und konzeptuelle Element überwiegt. Da man davon ausgehen kann, dass in etwas mehr als einem Jahrzehnt die Hälfte der Weltbevölkerung in Städten leben wird, ist es sehr wahrscheinlich, dass diese Art von privatem Garten in der Zukunft vorherrschen wird.

Les jardins privés, et en particulier ceux qui sont de dimensions réduites, situés, pour la plupart, en milieu urbain, sont étroitement liés à l'architecture, puisqu'elle les délimite, les structure et les définit. En fonction des proportions et de l'implantation au sein de l'édifice, il est possible d'établir des typologies très diverses déterminant les fonctions ultérieures : jardin, terrasse, balcon, jardin suspendu, patio, jardin frontal, etc. Toutefois, dû à des conditions rarement idéales et à l'accélération du rythme de la vie urbaine, limitant le temps disponible pour l'entretien des plantes, il existe aujourd'hui une typologie applicable à tous les cas : le jardin avec une prépondérance d'éléments inertes, à savoir, de l'architecture elle-même sur la végétation. Certains éléments naturels, qui en général nécessitent peu d'entretien, permettent de créer un jardin architectural où le concept et la forme sont les protagonistes. Vu que l'on estime que d'ici une décennie, la moitié de la population de la planète vivra dans des centres urbains, il est très probable que ce type d'espace vert devienne le jardin du futur.

Los jardines privados, y en especial aquellos que tienen dimensiones reducidas y ubicados, en su mayoría, en entornos urbanos, están estrechamente ligados a la arquitectura, ya que ésta los delimita, los estructura y les otorga su carácter primario. Dependiendo de sus proporciones y situación dentro del propio edificio, se pueden establecer tipologías muy variadas y que determinan las posteriores actuaciones: jardín, terraza, balcón, jardín colgante, patio, antejardín, etc. Sin embargo, debido a que las condiciones no suelen ser las apropiadas y a que el acelerado ritmo de vida urbano no permite disponer de mucho tiempo para el cuidado de la vegetación, actualmente existe una tipología aplicable a todas las anteriores: el jardín en el que predominan los elementos inertes, es decir, la propia arquitectura, sobre la vegetación. Por medio de ciertos elementos naturales, que por lo general exigen poco mantenimiento, se crea un jardín arquitectónico con una gran carga formal y conceptual. Puesto que se estima que dentro de algo más de una década la mitad de la población del planeta vivirá en centros urbanos, es muy probable que éste sea el tipo de jardín privado que predomine en el futuro.

I giardini privati, in special modo quelli di piccole dimensioni, ubicati per la maggior parte nei centri urbani, sono strettamente legati all'architettura, poiché questa li delimita, li struttura e conferisce loro un carattere dominante. A seconda delle loro proporzioni e della loro situazione all'interno dell'edificio, si possono stabilire tipologie molto diverse che determineranno i posteriori interventi: giardino, terrazza, balcone, giardino pensile, patio, giardino sul davanti, eccetera. Tuttavia, poiché le condizioni non sono di solito le più appropriate e il frenetico ritmo di vita urbano non lascia a disposizione molto tempo per prendersi cura della vegetazione, attualmente esiste una tipologia di giardino che può adattarsi a tutte quelle menzionate anteriormente: il giardino in cui predominano gli elementi inerti, vale a dire, l'architettura stessa e non la vegetazione. Con l'aiuto di alcuni elementi naturali, che in genere richiedono poca manutenzione, si crea un giardino architettonico con un grande peso formale e concettuale. Visto che si stima che tra circa un decennio la metà della popolazione mondiale abiterà in centri urbani, è molto probabile che, nel futuro, sia questo il tipo predominante di giardino privato.

Doctor Gabka Residential House Garden

Landscape design: Landau & Kindelbacher Architekten - Innenarchitekten
Location: Munich, Germany
Photography: Michael Heinrich